Opposing

By Catherine McNulty
Catalina Valenty

Thank you!

I just want to take a moment to thank everyone who has been so supportive, throughout this process. Your supportive words have meant so much to me.

I hope these poems bring you moments of self reflection or maybe a moment of personal or universal insight.

The arts have always been something I admired and enjoyed. To bring together my love of writing and photography into a book brings a great sense of accomplishment.

This is a collection of poems that are meant to be read top to bottom and bottom to top. When read in the opposite direction there is meant to be an opposing idea or concept within the poem, this was done in hopes that the reader would also take a moment to reflect on their lives.

The photographs are meant to compliment the theme of the poem and have a congruent theme of night skies and moons. The night skies are also meant to show that it is often during nightfall we find our selves deep in thought, while the moons are meant to represent the passage of time.

Table of Contents

Understanding Backwards

I am what he was.

He was the worst,

don't tell me that

The cleaning and reading everyday—wasn't so bad,

even though

that's what is left to remember.

Good memories shining through here and there,

your face in books.

I see you there,

to say you'er never here—

it would be a lie.

Day to Night

She gleams

night after night

her crown is decorated with silver and chrome

Her home;

a refuge of glinting diamonds and hazy dreams

Filled with secrets.

Night after night

she rises.

The swells and pulls of the night call and

with it, an infatuation of

the moon.

Singing Always

There once was a caged bird that sang for freedom

Feet no longer bound and within

a racing heart

she runs with

clipped wings and still she sings for freedom.

There will be a day without

clipped wings.

Fears of not making it because of

what she does not have are

always on her mind.

The ones in the future seem to be forever waiting and

one day there will be no need for this.

Hopefully…

There was Once

Again.

A compassionate and caring heart

once again shrouded by

shaken perspectives bubbling up to the surface,

time lost to hazy conversations and memories

through mumbled words and,

you were always there

with you, things were fine and

to be honest with myself,

would be to drown in insecurities.

Always bartering and fighting

with capsules of promises and bottled joy.

I desperately wish I didn't need to strike these deals,

No more.

Can I

I want to do it.

Just wait,

how can I

continue?

No desire to

be a failure.

Try to entertain the possibility that I will not…

I tell myself

I'm not enough,

as my heart pounds in my ears, intrusive thoughts say

consider the "what ifs…"

I shouldn't

but what if

I can.

You Without Me

I am more than this.

What I am,

you are not.

We are forever intertwined but separate,

promises were really made.

I suppose no more

sleepless nights, overthinking, and broken promises

Will appear only to be buried under

small rips and tears in my memories

I'm sorry for

everything.

Knew Once

For things I wish, I knew

Have an unnerving grip that holds my thoughts captive

more than once, allusive scents

bring me to you.

Still, there is a hidden craving for what may

not be there.

A gluttonous indulgence that can

only reside in hopeful daydreams.

Things I may have once known,

Things I may have invited.

They were once more than a whispered desire.

A victim yearning for tattooed smoke.

Longing for what has always been, and will forever be

Out of my reach.

Scared

I want to see what you see.

I wish to see that beauty within a lifetime.

An accumulation of markings are sometimes intentional and sometimes

Unintentionally made.

Assumptions of my character and values are

things that never seem to fade.

These are

what you see,

my fears are

my doubts

my faults

my scars

I am scared.

Could You

Within my deepest daydreams,

There is a promise to be there,

Through endless starry nights…

Wait, will you be patient?

Close your eyes,

And imagine if my words were dreams , you would sleep more.

If my desires and wishes were hidden under the night sky, I hope

You looked and truly tried to find them.

As shooting stars are silently streaming across the night sky

Within that silence

I hoped

You could understand.

I realized

You understood.

Place to Place

Once more,

Everything has become so wondrously new.

The sights and sounds of the familiar are made new

and yet,

again

There is an unknown anxious displeasure that always seems to follow

Once again,

For what was new becomes familiar and safe.

I have to grow to make room

for this.

A new place,

a new home,

a new name,

and again

I always crave it.

A shock that is extravagantly addictive.

I Did

There had been a hero.

As children we dreamed,

Once upon a time,

there was a hero.

Our eyes widened with wonder and amazement as

we admired honor., bravery,

responsibility and accountability seemed to be an absolute requirement.

Throwing away

Fear and panic for an innocent stranger.

How could you do that? Always having

To think,

Is it a threat?

Is it an immediate danger?

In a single moment there is no hesitation,

As you're constantly rushing in.

All this and still you are someone's hero and loved one.

Enough Now

Everyone knows and loves her, but not all of her.

We often crave to know more and more about her.

Only during special occasions

she is welcomed.

For her music and beauty,

for her food and fashion,

for her traditions,

she is celebrated and desired

Often to the point of excess.

They take in the name of admiration and take

to be changed

to be renamed

They seemed like they wanted everything,

Just not her.

Only the culture that raised and created her.

Please Wait

I am thankful for having known you,

And for those moments

When "goodbye" is not easy,

When saying "I miss you,"

Just doesn't seem like it will be enough.

Saying three little words…

Seems too small to be encompassed by

everything we've done together,

A short bittersweet sorrowful goodbye to

a space in my heart,

and things that will forever be in

My memories.

Within Opposing Commonalities

The cycle begins.

Once more,

It passes and as we live

there is no clear beginning and yet

like sand running through our fingers,

it shows no signs of slowing or showing us an end.

I gave birth to everything wicked and divine,

Woven through countless secrets, stars, and memories,

I was and am eternal mutability.

I am cyclical and at times cynical,

But you, are also the reason I am loved and praised.

You exist so that others may know my worth.

I am life and it is time that defines us all.

Life, death, and time.

Thank you!

I just want to take a moment to thank everyone who has been so supportive, throughout this process. Your supportive words have meant so much to me.

I hope these poems bring you moments of self reflection or maybe a moment of personal or universal insight.

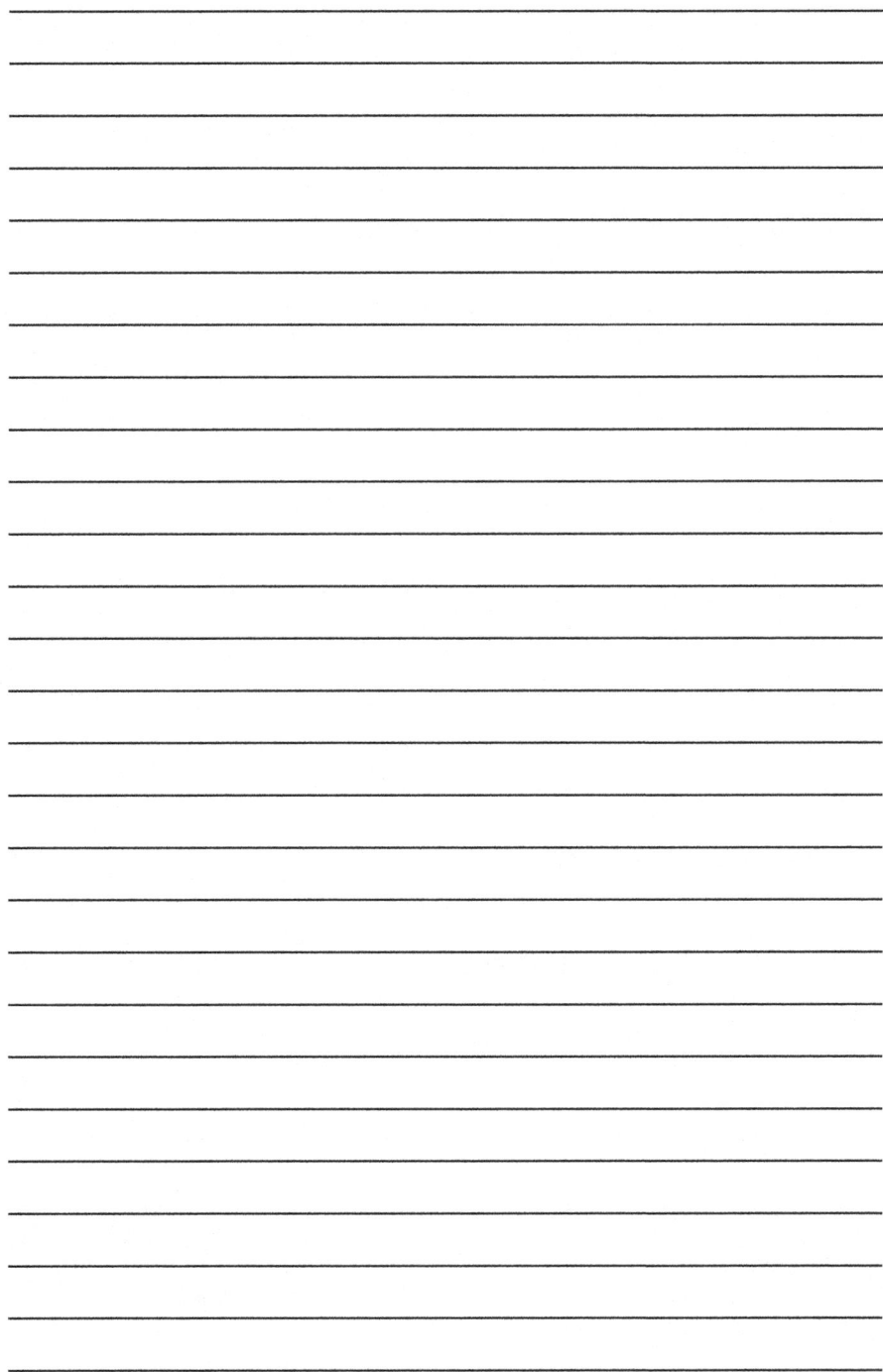

Made in the USA
Las Vegas, NV
23 April 2021

21931499R00056